Silence Is Consent

Rosemary Winderlich

Silence Is Consent

Silence Is Consent
ISBN 978 1 76041 848 9
Copyright © text Rosemary Winderlich 2020

First published 2020 by
Ginninderra Press
PO Box 3461 Port Adelaide 5015
www.ginninderrapress.com.au

Contents

Foreword	9
Going under?	11
A nation of boat people	12
Refugee Policy	13
In the camp	14
Beyond grief	15
Perhaps tomorrow	16
My daughter	17
Why are you hiding?	18
Fearful memories	19
Porn on my Facebook	20
Your child, my child	21
Talk, talk, talk	22
No small thing	23
Soul pain	24
My wish for you	25
Voices calling	26
Change will come	27
Sleeping giant, wake up!	28
Young men dream	29
In the wild	30
A ray of light	31
Your own words judge you	33
On signing petitions	35
Fireflies	36
Interview on Al Jazeera	37
Some positivity please	38
Lessons from Sudoku	39
Heads bowed	40
Rainy day in Singapore	41

Deeper into the dunghill	42
Welcome centre at Norwood	44
This sad world	46
I am sorry	47
Forcibly moved	48
While I stand here	49
Wake up!	50
Silence is consent	51
Wake in fright	52
Heading north to Siassi	53
Trails of tears	54
Never again	56
My Birthday celebrations	58
Finding a balance	59
To all in detention	60
Ghouta is not dead	61
Garden in the ruins: Syria	62
Beneath Syrian streets	63
One small dot	64
The heavens weep	65
That shameful day: April 2018	66
After High Court Decision, April 2019	67
Present pain	68
Obscene!	69
For the Rohingya	70
Shamim	71
No logic	72
Amendments Again? 2018	74
Dark-eyed girl	75
Sleeping giant	76
Playing games?	77
Death of a spirit	78

Little brown boy	79
Never alone	80
Fear in the night	81
Tender Age Shelters: 19.5.18	82
The tide will turn	84
My inspired new solution	85
Dare you?	87
One ordinary person	88
Tears for the Hazara	89
Refugee mother to her child	90
Port Ashmore: a comedy?	91
Forced removal, again	93
At Christmas	94
Frozen Rose	95
Another new year	96
Beyond imagining	97
Homeless	98
Through the night	99
Climate change	100
Anyone watching?	102
Should I intrude?	103
Money, money, money	104
False news?	105
Seesaw and swings	106
To a baby boy	107
Child sacrifice	108
It's beginning!	109
Ageing	110
Unwanted	111
War for our world	112
Will I let you live?	114
Medevac Bill passed!	115

Morning check of Facebook	118
The human condition	120
At last!	121
Where is my baby?	122
The stars look down	123
Violent times	125
Alone	126
The voice of Australia	127
Prayer for those in darkness	128
Unleash compassion	129
How can this happen?	130
Three women of Iran	131
Inland night	132

Foreword

These poems are my response to a disgraceful chapter of Australian history.

Friends on Manus and Nauru, and in detention elsewhere, I feel pain and despair for your suffering, but I have not personally experienced your situation, so please forgive me if sometimes I do not reflect your experience well, or seem to belittle your pain. I mean to be respectful. I am careful about sources, and try to avoid sensationalising. Please forgive my mistakes.

I feel strongly that we must all be ready to speak up, no matter what the cost, because…

…silence is consent.

Going under?

Australia, land of the free, of opportunity
spiralling out of control, regressing
diet of careful lies blinding our eyes
deadening sensibilities
false promises created to demoralise
deals and tricks…so much to hide
devolving into a dictatorship
ruled by secrecy, self-interest.
Where are we going but downhill fast?
What will we be when we get there?

Land down under going under
slipping down down
between layers of sewage and waste.
What a sad waste!

Hold on, hold on to shreds of decency.
We can, we can claw back, crawl back
up the disgusting slide of deceit and cruelty
denial, avoidance of responsibility.
We can climb back to honesty and dignity
free Australia fair, wounded, desecrated
buried down there, where dark things hide
dirtied and scarred, blinded by lies
but still a sleeping conscience deep inside.

Wake up! Climb up with me!
Break our chains by setting others free.

A nation of boat people

My heart full of others' pain –
a pale reflection of their pain.
Can't sleep…so much sadness, deceit
children exploited in this century?

The Industrial Revolution
no work, thieves hung
or sent around the world as convicts
for stealing to feed their children
then Scottish and Irish enclosures
land stolen by the rich.

One grandfather came as a missionary.
Austrian, German, Polish, Danish
in my family tree, now all Australians
then ten-pound Poms, Jews, Greeks, Italians
Balts, and more, all dispossessed by war.
Then the Asian flow from nearer wars
most now valuable citizens.
Further back in time, archeologists say
there were three waves of Aboriginals
some over land bridge, some by canoes
the first boat people, the first Australians.

So here we are, a nation of boat people
all contributing to a wonderful diversity
still some inequalities and tensions
but a rich nation, with space to share.
Why can't we welcome more?

Refugee Policy

Our rotten migrant policy is battering Australia
gradually indoctrinating in the threat of difference
hardening the perpetrators, damaging their souls
teaching cruelty and indifference to our own children
who understand more than we give them credit for
and will probably grow up to do as we have done.

Amendments enacted to protect our politicians
loopholes shut and freedoms curtailed
impossible to recognise the old, fair Australia.
What have we become?

Perhaps our politicians believe they are protecting us
perhaps convince themselves they deserve our thanks?
I believe with all my heart they are damaging our future
creating a generation that will follow in their footsteps.
Kindness and justice will continue to diminish
so the world we leave our children will be very different
from the era we have lived in
sadly
more like a dictatorship.

In the camp

Child's eyes question
Why? Why?

Time passes
blossom dries
fries in white heat
forty degrees or more
in barren camp.

A tropical island
climate ideal
while away hours
relax by the pool
frangipani and hibiscus flowers
under wide spreading trees
soft breeze through leaves
peaceful and cool.

Not where the children are
no shade, sun burns
no shady trees, no ferns
heat harsh
mineral sands reflect sun
hot air, hot feet.

Hearts empty
nerves unravel.

Hope dies.

Beyond grief

Unwanted, forgotten
agonising for their children
grasping distant hope
for their children
believing hope still shines
in blue infinity up there
and somewhere
is safety for the children.

Broken promises
treacherous steps to climb
dark tunnels to negotiate
to where?
Anywhere. Elsewhere.
Thrust trust into a vacuum
step into the unknown
clasping the children.

Reward for courage, initiative…
more rejection
punishment for existence
punishment for hope.

Where is a place to relax and know
the children can play and grow
a place for them to rest and be
safe from reprisals and the cruel sea?

Perhaps tomorrow

a lullaby

Sleep, my son, for I am here
and will be as long as I can.
Sleep, my child, and do not fear
my precious little man.

Sleep and dream of a better day
water so you can have a bath
clouds to keep the hot sun away
perhaps the first step on a better path.

Sleep now, sleep, my little one
at last the night is cool and still
another sad hot day has gone
and tomorrow another will.

Sleep, my child, so I can weep
let despair contort my face
for your uncertain future here
for the cruelty of the human race

Sleep, my son, and I will pray
for help from our God above
that people everywhere will soon
turn again to love.

My daughter

My sweet daughter, almost grown
hair of silk, lustrous eyes
but please, my daughter
hide your eyes, look down
hide your sweet smile, please frown.
You long to be beautiful…you are
to preen, brush your hair and dream
but pack those dreams away.
They do not fit our life today.

My daughter, you long to be admired
but not now, not now.
If some guard, nicer than the rest
offers you gifts, beckons you near
don't go…don't go.
Hide your beautiful eyes, sweet smile
let your hair hang unbrushed.
My sweet child, my beautiful girl
I long to keep you safe.

Your sister drowned, your brother too
your father beheaded years ago
you are my treasure, all I have.
Take care. Take care.
Please hide your beauty and grace
until we can leave this place
just for this while
so I can keep you safe, my dear.

Why are you hiding?

Why are you hiding there, little sister
why are you hiding behind the curtain?
The sun is shining, the children are here.
Come out and play.

I am afraid of the stares of the strangers.
I am afraid of the eyes of the guard.
I have seen little girls hurting and crying
so I will stay here.

Why are you hiding your eyes, my sweet mother
why do you cover you beautiful face?
Why don't you laugh and play with me, mother
as you once did?

If I smile, the guards might notice me
and follow when I go to bathe.
The look in their eyes frightens me
so I hide my smiles.

Why are you hiding your face, my father
why are you eyes turned to the ground?
I can remember your eyes full of laughter.
Why always look down?

If I look in the eyes of the guard, I see hate.
If I look in the eyes of my wife, I see shame.
In the eyes of my children, such sadness…
so I look down.

Fearful memories

I have memories to comfort me
when family are far apart
warm me when life seems cold
and as I grow old
these treasures well up in my heart

What memories will these
child refugees, hold in their hearts?
Memories of dark despair
of families torn apart?

What memories will they have
of a happy childhood home
What model of parenting
seeing parents impotent?

When justice is finally done
and they find a home at last
will we punish them again
because they have no warm memories
on which to build their parenting?
Because of all they've lost
their little ones might doubly pay the cost
of Australia's cruelties.

A gift of fearful memories.

Porn on my Facebook

Privacy violated.
I am ashamed for those who see it
feel dirty, disillusioned
complacency gone.

Child in the camp, though averting eyes
sees mother degraded, sister humiliated
spied on by staff
hears insolent tones, abusive language
learns about violence, abuse of power
these lessons staining minds of children
detained in our name.
The word Australia to them
means fear, anger, pain.

What are we doing, in our silences
training our victims to victimise others
imprinting images impossible to delete
teaching them to follow the steps of suppressors
a cycle of hate in which we each play our part
each time we look the other way
each time we are silent when we should speak
– producing terrorists?

Your child, my child

Look into your child's eyes
raised in trust to you
see your child's smile.

Now try, try to see another child
same size, on crowded ship
food, water running out
or under fire year after year
stench of death, no smiles.

Listen to your child laugh
play happily, secure in your love
knowing you will meet his needs
then try, in your mind's eye, your heart
to see another child, same size
hiding in rubble, listening to guns
fleeing in panic, fearing our bombs
sleeping, freezing on the streets
of countries they trusted for justice
imprisoned behind barbed wire
too weak to play in the tropical sun
thirsty, water strictly rationed.
Perhaps some tomorrow…try to imagine.

Can you try to clear your mind
of the supposed threat they pose
clear the careful lies from your eyes
see a child, much like your child.

Can't you weep for that child?

Talk, talk, talk

You can talk of threats to Australian security
you can talk of principles, threats to the economy
you can vent your anger in vicious conversation
to discredit the other party or nation.

Talk, talk, talk. Please, let's make it positive.
It's simple: we all know the Golden Rule
and most parents try to practise affirmation.
Why can't we try to follow those practices
in our discussions about the current situation?

Hmm…so…
must try to find something positive to say
about those who hide truth, send helpless babes away.
Try this: Indonesians who transported asylum seekers
were possibly in need, and have been well rewarded
by our government, for turning back to Indonesia.

Perhaps we could say thank you to our mighty leaders
for rudeness to our Human Rights Commission president
as this has emphasised everything she stands for?
– a rather negative kind of positivity.

Let's avoid name calling, try to speak constructively
(though it is satisfying to have a good grumble).

No small thing

When we returned from years in the tropics
there were many adjustments to be made
warm clothes needed, shoes, socks, coats.
Our younger children needed assistance
tying shoelaces, seldom wore shoes there.

Our children's skin was yellow from quinine
their different accent, customs, only slowly accepted.

Then there was water.
On our mountainous island, rivers always flowed
rain roared in most days from the sea.
Here we daily reminded *please switch off the tap*.

We watched them carefully for culture shock,
tried to provide support and understanding
during the stressful days of relocation.
We showered two or three times a day up there
sticky heat, perspiration, which of course
must be replaced by drinking more water.

This morning as I luxuriated in my hot shower
I thought of those mothers now in detention
perhaps, perhaps today a shower permitted
if they show their bodies for the privilege.

Perhaps it seems a simple thing
but there, it's serious, life-threatening
in tropical heat, to have limited water
– no small thing.

Soul pain

I have a pain deep in my soul
for my country, rich and beautiful
a sickness in its core.

The men of Manus wait in fear
have waited long, with dignity
facing petty persecution
and can't take much more.

How can this happen in this age
disease of hate, fear, pride
overcoming humanity.
I have a pain deep inside.
Families intentionally separated
little children abused, tortured
parents powerless.

There is a pain in my soul
my country demeaned, disgraced
a deadly infection
consciously fostered to spread and grow
and overthrow humanity and integrity.

This cannot happen but it is happening.

There is a heavy pain
and there is shame deep in my soul.

My wish for you

(to a refugee)

I wish for you a moment
between traumas and fears
I wish for you a time to smile
though through tears
to remember happiness
with family
perhaps rich village life
before catastrophe
your children's happy play
before their eyes grew sad
tender times with your true love
before he disappeared.

I pray this sad time will pass
and you will find a home
and so much more
but just for now
I wish for you a piece of time
when you can smile
rest in sweet memories
just for a while.

Voices calling

Through the night their voices call to me
through the night their faces stay with me
little children struggling in the sea…
they call my name.

Through the day their voices call to me
the young men struggling to be free
their voices pleading for humanity…
they call my name.

Through the day their voices call to me
children detained unjustly here
in their own land imprisoned cruelly…
they call my name

and as each time their voices fade and die
as they go down into obscurity
in the sea of our insecurity
new voices rise.

This wonderful country, wide and free
drowns in our own inhumanity
deaf to the cries of those in misery
rising to the skies.

Change will come

Feeling weight of lost hopes
groaning over the sea
their hopelessness, sorrow
for their children's tomorrow.
Will they ever be free?

I hear decency stirring
waking from slumber
consciences waking
awareness rising.
All around this land
embers are fanned.

As fire reborn from a single spark
to burn the dross and light the dark
as spring buds, bursts and blooms
as babies grow in mother's wombs
change must come.

Change will come.

Sleeping giant, wake up!

Soon, soon the sleeping giant will rise
while the monster of Deceit
sated by lies and blighted lives
will lie defenceless, easy prey…
perhaps today?
Proponents of violence and lies
you have long had your say
now tangled, tied in your own web
your time is done.
It's past time for your demise.

Now is the time to open our eyes
see where truth lies
Be strong. Stand up and say
It was wrong, we were wrong,
to define those who came to us
as expendable, inferior
see them as enemies.

It's late
so much hate has grown
hate spawned of fear
and we must own
our terrible injustices

Lord, forgive our apathy…
we tried not to see.

Young men dream

Young men dream dreams
of position, power, love and glory
perhaps surfing, or soaring the skies
architecture, mathematics
each dreams his story
– a powerful motorbike
riding the wind, his love behind him
a home, children laughing, playing
his fields, his business prospering.
Young men dream dreams.

Can dreams live behind prison walls ?
They fade, fade to bare survival
then another dreamer falls
hopes fail, he falls.

In a climate of fear and hate
how can dreams live
dreams of a useful life without fear
dreams of a future with us here
of what they can give?
Another dreamer falls.

Beware, beware what we give
our own young ones.
Inoculated with fear and hate
what dreams will they dream?
What have we done?

In the wild

Off the highway, down a side track
under the overpass, way out back
behind facade of civilised lives
bitumen roads, boundary fences
ordered rows of wheat or vines
into the wild, where dingoes roam
snakes and lizards make their home
invisible agents of decay eat heart wood away.

Behind the myth of Australia Fair
greed rules. We are pawns to manipulate
each only a tool for political gain.
Transparency dies on the altar of lies
sacrificed for power. Corruption thrives
the innocent lost in forests of innovations
too convoluted to unravel
spores settle unseen, cancer grows
we struggle to swim against the flow.

Don't the powerful know, surely they know
their protective policies will cause their own demise.
Don't they see, they themselves
have destroyed ways of retreat, bridges burned
undermined foundations of their position
and even worse, their children are conditioned
to be cruel and ruthless in their turn.

Surely deep in the wild, under the compost
protected from storms above
slowly waking and unfurlng, there are still
tender new shoots of humanity and love.

A ray of light

They say, give me the child
until he is three, or is it four.
I'm not sure…
perhaps in general outlook
perhaps in philosophy
but not fixed in attitude
or why
do Siassi music, drums sweep in
fill my heart to overflowing
Batak pipes and harmonies
override childhood immersion
in European harmonies
and mean so much to me?
Words in Saveng, Mbula, Indonesian
come first to my tongue
before my birth language?

And how, why
can a narrow spirit, well taught
bloom and change
or siblings, close in age, grow to be
very different in philosophy?

So, teach your children well
but don't underestimate
the strength of a later socialisation.

And there's a ray of light!
Hope in dark night!

Victims of violence
young ones incarcerated
slaves dehumanised
children fearfully abused
hopefully
can be healed significantly
(though never completely)
if steeped in respect and love.

Do you have love to give?

Your own words judge you

What can I say to you, smiling on the screen
but shame, shame, shame…
yours, which you must feel deep inside
but stuck in mire of lies cannot escape.
My shame that I have not done more
and shame on Australia's name.

Your expression, unfeeling, emotionless
just as well. Without imposed control
your emotions would shout, not be denied
wear you out, tear you inside.
Each challenge you rebut, though evidence clear
disregarding any view that disagrees with you.
I will pray for your sad heart, full of hidden fear.

Bland face, harsh words but surely turmoil inside.
How can you convince yourself, hide
your intentional cruelty, disdain for human life
frequent changes of policy just to increase
human discomfort and humiliation?
From your mouth flow words, words, words
platitudes, generalisations, fabrications
meaningless words demeaning our nation.

So ridiculous, so wasteful and meaningless
When will this grim charade cease?
Generous benefactor of refugees?
Orderly migration programme? Oh please!
Open your eyes and heart. This vile disease
will destroy this land, riddled with corruption
a contagious disease
encouraged by our leaders' inhumanities.

Words flow on, flow on, flow on
credibility long gone.

On signing petitions

Each one of us is only one
but if we hope, pray, scream for action
if our hearts are despairing, crying
for children mutilated, dying
families fractured, lives distorted
for those seeming beautiful and whole
with deep wounds in their soul
we will sign.

Perhaps you laugh at me, cringe at my naivety
even unfriend me, still I will post and sign.
If we discount the worth of one voice, yours or mine
how can we expect change on this struggling earth
encrusted with corruption and shame?
If we cringe in fear of ridicule, of looking political
who will speak for those without a voice?
If I withhold my one small voice, and so do you
then who will speak for the dispossessed?
Come, stand with me and say
there is a much better way.

If we are brave, stand together, and sign
we can be a dam to stop the tainted wave.
Add your small light to mine
Soon more and more will shine
to warm the imprisoned, the refugee
let them see they are not alone in their dark night.
We cannot stop until the suffering are free.

Until then I will speak and post and write
and I will sign.

Fireflies

Behind the aid post, down by the river
a firefly tree
a mango, I think.

On quiet tropical nights, a fairy tree
syncopated rhythm, dancing, changing
Christmas lights sparkling continually.

We caught a few fireflies, carefully
little bugs, unimpressive
covered them and peeped to see…
yes, a small glow, but on the tree
in dark night
dazzling, mesmerising.

Each of us might seem ordinary
but working together
when all is dark around
we can create dazzling delight
or at least a little comfort
in someone's dark night.

Interview on Al Jazeera

2016

I am sorry for you.
Many little promises, perhaps you didn't really mean
many little trades and ties, not quite scrupulously clean
concessions here and there, mates' networks everywhere
just smooth the way, bring perks…
is that the way it works
in politics?

Gradually, sneakily, those little promises and ties
twist into strong threads, then ropes. You realise
now they must be hidden by more compromise
and bigger lies.

So the net is woven, from threads not quite clean
then ropes increasingly dirty and obscene
until a filthy web is there, a trap to catch you unaware
because of that first compromise, first little lie
those nods and handshakes, scratch my back

now you are trapped, paralysed
by all those slightly unwise ties
cannot follow your own conscience
afraid to make an honest stand
for fear of that net hanging over head.

Obviously compromised
not the leader now: now you are led.

Some positivity please

Mind tight with the plight of children in detention
the homeless, overlooked, repressed
what else can I write when my heart is sore
children abused and so much more
though that's what I didn't mean to mention

I'll try…
Cold rainy grey day today
but suddenly, a golden ray.
In summer we long for a shady place
wear hats, sunscreen on our face
the sun is an enemy
but in winter we welcome the sun
sweet relief from the chill and cold
soften the day with a touch of gold
the reign of winter is almost done

Now in winter, the sun is a friend
telling us the reign of cold will end
there will be warmth and peace again
there will be love and peace again.

Hearts and minds will mend
slowly mend.

Lessons from Sudoku

Petitions, appeals, save a life, end a war…

I am one very small drop in the ocean
one insignificant voice.
Can I end slave labour, help the abused
protect threatened species
fight for resources misused?

Sudoku, sometimes frustrating
but keep trying, keep trying
one number found can turn all around
magically many more slot into place.
At first seems unsolvable
then
each number slips sweetly into its space.

So as heartbreaking causes
pop up on my screen, I remember
just one little number, one small voice
can make a difference,
influence a vote, a choice.

A small thing, a very small thing
but a thing we can do, me and you.
So keep assessing, questioning
thoughtfully acting or signing…

something anyone can do.

Heads bowed

(waiting for result of Parliament's decision)

Heads bowed today
praying for humane decision.
Then heads bowed
disbelief and heavy pain
crying, hopes fading
weariness of years trying
to bring their families to safety
the pain of daily struggle
demeaning conditions
being seen as nothing
not worthy fellow humans.

And yet
through heaped losses they speak sweetly
even respectfully, to us, their oppressors
and still Australia fails to see their humanity.

We bow our heads now
pray for the despairing that they don't despair
for the oppressors that they open their hearts
that when they do, shame will not break them

and especially today, heads bowed, for the children
pray they will still know forgiveness and hope
not be brutalised by their harsh existence.

We bow in shame that this can happen in our name.
pray for strength to stand, to band together and say
Give them a place, secure and safe
help them stand again in dignity.

Rainy day in Singapore

A peaceful day
quiet rain falling in Brossard Street
gentle rain, of patience and persistence
slowly erodes prison walls, unjust laws
but too slow, too slow.
The children can't wait. Send a storm
urgency and action needed now
fierce storm, tumult breaking dams
breaking walls.

Not far across the sea, Rohingya flee.
Not far to the east, detention on Battam.
In Jakarta, Pekan Baru, people like me and you
lives suspended, waiting, waiting.

My heart is heavy for you, bowed with sorrow
long suffering, frustration, despair
dying hopes for a better tomorrow
though I cannot fully understand.
I am not you. I am not there.

Morning check of Facebook, what you say
from those bare, harsh prisons far away
weighs my heart down with shame.
More injustice every day, a cruel game.

We pray for strength to stand and say
Stop all this prevarication
There is only one reasonable solution.
Bring them here.

Deeper into the dunghill

Just how I feel, no pretty way to say it.

Deeper deeper into the dunghill
deeper deeper into the mire
ignorance, apathy, selfishness
but more shameful than these
consciously turning our backs
on the chaos our leaders created
denying our responsibilities.

Quagmire of lies and righteous denials
cunningly constructed, compounded
recipes for destruction of fellow humans
orchestrated dehumanising, vilifying
those our nation has wrongly imprisoned
thumbing our nose at world censure
in cowardice cunningly dumping our mess
our secret sins and webs of deceit
on smaller nations nearby
leaving them to carry our shame
struggle out from under our pile of mire.

And I can't believe it.
In my country
brutality to children
perhaps wayward, destructive
but still children
isolated, brutalised
their well paid carers
poisoning their victims' futures.

Greyhounds and exported cows
more important than children in detention
our country's morality skewed, distorted
dishonour endemic throughout our nation.

Not our responsibility? Wash our hands?
Continue obliviously on our privileged way?
It will all come back to bite us, one day.

A new morning…
where is the hope dawning
for those we imprison, repress and deny
and for our suffering, declining, nation
terminally ill?

Lord, you are there, you care.
Show us a way to climb back
to sunlight once more.

Welcome centre at Norwood

Refuge of warmth and love where hope can rise again.

Last week, a young Afghani man, new trained barista
smiling proudly, served me coffee.
A woman hugged me, tears falling
Your son has been so good to me she said.
A young woman sat with me, seemed confident, friendly.
She came two months ago from Christmas Island.
Her little son is noisy. Wakes often in the night
A knock on the door, he screams *Is it Immigration?*
She seems surprised that we don't criticise.

How much time until he recovers peace of mind?
Even small traumas can have lasting effects.
These have seen what children should never see.

A young man sits with us, two years detained in Darwin
wary, not meeting our eyes. Later he talks compulsively.
Governments are all the same, care only about money.
His mouth smiles, not his eyes.
The word *Nauru* is whispered quietly, fearfully.

The room hums: tutors, law student help with documents
volunteers serve lunch, then announcements.
A friend was seized last night, flown to detention in Perth.
It was the smiling boy who made coffee.

Silence. *It might be me next time…*
not safe even here, even here.

Talk resumes, all seem calm, though any day
they might be violently returned to the dangers they fled.
They thank me warmly…for a little interest?

I am ashamed of the misery my country inflicts
deliberately.

This sad world

This world…what can I say?
Horrors multiply day by day.
We must, we must all stand and say
there is a better way.

All who sit secure, life safe and sweet
perhaps for now escape the heat
the terror, horror and defeat, beware!
We all must feel another's pain
we all must fight to cleanse the stain
or oppression will grow insidiously
burn us all with its deadly glare.

The despairing mother in deadly fear
violence and rape very near
fighting to protect what is most dear
is sister, daughter to you and me.
Hopeless, helpless, anguished men
cannot protect their little children
those they struggled to bring this far
following hope and freedom's star
dreams undone by our harsh policies.

Our responsibility, our privilege
to fight for children who know no peace
where wars never cease and children here
harshly dealt with in their helplessness
needlessly imprisoned and oppressed.

Come, let's fight for people like us
children like ours
caught in war's inhumanity
our privilege, our responsibility.

I am sorry

(On deleting from my emails)

There is too much war, destruction, sorrow.
I can cry for some and write and post
and I try, but there is too much, too much
too many children lost, mistreated, dying
women abused, beaten, refugees fleeing
too much screaming, despair, crying.

No one can absorb it all – at least, not me.
Forgive me. Your pain is real. I respect it
but one person cannot support each cause
weep for each, pray for each
so each of us can only do our best
trust others for the rest.

This sad, sad world is groaning
I can hear the weeping, moaning
too much for me to carry.
Forgive me, I am sorry (delete, delete, delete)
I can only follow some.

You will not notice my absence
my inaction at your sorrow
your urgent cause, but I know
and feel guilt as I delete, delete
because there is only so much
one person can absorb and follow.
I leave you in God's hands and pray
pray, pray for a better tomorrow.

I respect your fear and sorrow
but delete, delete, delete. I am sorry.

Forcibly moved

(November 2017)

I'm mad, I'm sad
head tight, heart bleeding inside
want to scream, cry, fight.

The video rolls on and on
abuse, threats, shouting
hard-won food destroyed
growing things trampled
clever water sinks destroyed
no safety, no guarantees
just more humiliation.

Guards use privilege and might
to abuse, ridicule
phones destroyed
can't contact family.
My head tight with their plight
our disgrace, our shame.

So to the garden to clear my head
breathe fresh air, plant corn, beans
in fruitful soil, and pray and trust
something of hope and beauty
will grow again in them
that they will not give up.

Then back inside to post and tweet.

Have to do something.

While I stand here

As I stand here washing dishes
a small child far away
is abused, in pain and terror
knowing no one will help.
A refugee mother is raped
by those paid to protect her.

While we stand here arguing
about the threat of alien invasion
men in our refugee camps
write affirming, respectful letters to us.

While we stand back
blind to what is done in our name
it increases
because it seems we approve.

Perpetrators also are our victims
they believe we do not care
so we give them power
and power corrupts.

We are also victims
sensibilities deadening.

And I believe that we do care
so we must inform ourselves
stand for justice and humanity.

Each voice counts.

Wake up!

Wake up, Australia! Can't you see
the rot going on in the name of you and me
cruelty, child abuse, lies and secrecy?
It threatens to bury us forever.

Our name around the world is a dirty word.
What can we do to clear this blot?
It will take years but we must start
open our eyes, our ears, our hearts
so we can see that each refugee
whatever their politics, status, religion
is a human being, like you and me.
Whatever our colour or philosophy
respect others or we disrespect ourselves
because we are all human, aren't we?

So dig out that hidden sensitivity.
We all must have love hiding inside.
Try to imagine the heart of a mother
child drowned, abused before her eyes
and she powerless.
Try to imagine what a father is feeling
seeing his children suffer and die.

Please try. You know it's not right
this shameful oppression must cease
but it won't until each of us stands to fight
for justice, humanity and peace.

First step is simple: hold out your hand
say refugees are welcome here
and smiles are free.

Silence is consent

Speak up, Don't wait.
Today a young woman assaulted
a child abused, abusers unpunished
the innocent punished for fleeing injustice.

Try to imagine how a raped child feels
rapist still visible daily, in control.

Their danger is real
their degrading life is real
well documented, photographed
incriminating documents leaked
justice still blindfolded
no one prosecuted.

Imagine your daughter
your baby son,
your precious one
in such a place…
our disgrace.

It's up to us
to end this blight
this shame.
Speak up!
Sign your name!
Silence is consent.

Wake in fright

I wake in fright late at night
unseen demon lurking near
pause in breath, little death
no sound, breathless fear.

Breathe slow. Lord, I know
you are here, very near
never leave. Carry me
through the jungle of my fear.

Keyboard malfunction slows me down
a small thing, frustrating me.
Yes, too dependent on devices
now, cut off from escape route
from exorcising demons in words
another terror rises
greater helplessness.

Strategy two, transpose my fear
to those helpless and imprisoned
try to understand their plight.
How can they stay sane, waiting, waiting
transfixed by nails unknown, threatening
no resolution, no reunion in sight?

I breathe slow, wait for panic to subside
my little fear almost disabling me.

A very small thing, in comparison.

Heading north to Siassi

(Our home in PNG, 1965 to 1975)

On the threshold
between two worlds
Lae well behind us
Finschafen unseen on our left
surging north to Siassi.

Manus Island, further on,
crossroads of many worlds
already far behind me
old loves waiting further on
and heavy on my mind
weight of horror and shame
the bleak world of refugees
islands of grief and pain
just a few more hours north.

Mixed emotions
thankfulness in returning
and heart sick
at inhumanity unbelievable
rejoicing and mourning
fighting each other
as I near sweet reunions.

When will they see loved ones again?

Trails of tears

Zoom out: the world spreads wide below.
What are these scribbled lines on the snow
inching on through desert dust, jungle heat
edging ever forward, diminishing as they go
what are these ant trails?

Trails from lofty tower, babble of languages
unity disrupted, they headed out
seeking a new place of their own.
Long column of Israelites, fleeing slavery
God leading, clear goal, long road ahead.

Trails of tears cross this beautiful, skewed globe
the victories of exploration and expansion
often built on repression and dispossession
decimated Indian tribes herded to reservations
unconstitutional, breaking the treaty of 1835
the Five Nations
with their own democratic society
modern cities, libraries, newspapers, universities
their success perhaps undermining white supremacy
their Cherokee land was taken despite treaty
forced west through deep winter, 8,000 miles
4,000 deaths or more along the Trail of Tears
to Indian territory in Oklahoma.

Zoom in: innumerable laborious trails
survivors of gulags straggling home
and there are the Jews again
uprooted by pogroms, again, trails fanning out
looking for safety somewhere to start again
or on their way to the promised land.

Refugees of many wars still stagger, crawl, die
Back through time, we see continuing caravans
heavy with losses, dying hopes, struggling on.

A new one: the oppressed of middle America
migrant caravan from Honduras edging north
for freedom, for democracy.
Hopes betrayed, children seized, many not reunited.
Parents deported, leaving children in limbo
a comedy, if not such a tragedy.

And still in Africa ongoing streams
from beleaguered countries sketching their story
homes left, disease, death…lines of suffering
etched on the surface of this globe.

When will mankind learn we are one family?
Unless we work together, all will fall eventually.

Never again

As I roamed far and free in the sun
life full of and discovery and fun
death trains were rolling.
While we rode our bikes to school
the furnaces were burning.
Parents in Europe, in despair and fear
tried to avoid terrors still unclear
the truth gradually emerging.

Now, as my grandchildren play
confident of love and security
poisonous mist is rising
creeping, seeping in to our paradise
and just like then, not believing our eyes
that our land would so abuse fellowmen
the innocent, women, little children.

As Jewish parents prayed with fading hope
at last glimpsing the vast scope
of the planned genocide
as they calmed their children's fears
tried to keep hopes alive, through anguished tears
as they watched their children pale and die
by fellow humans abused and terrorised.

Does this sound familiar?

Now on Manus and Nauru, mental agony
as innocent prisoners look out over the sea
as time impassive, merciless, rolls on
their children's innocence and childhood gone
comforts maliciously withdrawn, one by one
each home made well broken, polluted
food, medicine cut off, electricity disconnected
no safety, no reasonable solution presented
…can you imagine…try to imagine.
what if this was your family, your wife, your child?

After that other inhumanity, mankind's shame
the world said resoundingly 'never again'
and now…we are doing much the same.

My Birthday celebrations

(2016)

Joyful gathering of friends and family
happy laughter surrounding me
but deep inside there is a place
of sadness, shame, disgrace
that my great country can oppress
those who come in hopefulness
that as I rejoice and celebrate
they suffer humiliation and pain
injustice so glaring, so great
while I celebrate.

Privileges, comforts all revoked
privacy, medical care denied
demeaned, punished, provoked
justice manipulated, mutilated.
Humanity has died.

A tightness in my throat
tears close behind my eyes
while I laugh and celebrate

they are with me.

Finding a balance

A glorious new day alive with birdsong.
I praise my Lord for many things
Meanwhile, in this peaceful moment
a child is abused in our prison camp
a mother must show her body
for water to wash her child
assaults reported, no one punished
continuing brutality, disrespect, rape.

A beautiful day
my heart rises, but not far
anchored by disgust and shame.
How can I rejoice in my freedom
when hate and cruelty reign?
Shame, such shame in Australia's name.

Eyes beseeching – what can I do?
I write letters, sign petitions.
It is not enough.
Rejoice in each new day?
A balance impossible to keep
weight of despair and horror
outweighing peace of mind
praising God for His goodness to me
while weeping for those who weep.

Lord, heal my country,
from this unbelievable inhumanity
set us free.

To all in detention

The middle of Christmas night, I sit awake
thinking of our happy Christmas gatherings
Adults reminiscing, children laughing
building memories, building family.

And where are your children?

Food, food, each brings their speciality
eating together integral to festivity.
We eat too much. What do you eat tonight
in that bare, harsh place, Australia's disgrace?

My eyes rest on my children, grandchildren
great-grandchildren, happy together
celebrating Jesus' birthday and the gifts he gives
and through the happiness, you are with me
in my heart, tears close behind my eyes.

I feel your longing for your family
for happy gatherings that used to be
for those lost needlessly on land or sea
or somewhere in the tangled tide
still seeking safety.
Through happy days, horror travels with me
thinking of your suffering, praying for you.
You are not forgotten.
Our Lord walks with you
weeps with you
every step of the weary way.

Ghouta is not dead

Ghouta, you are not dead
you have moved on
to highways, hidden tracks
leaving home weeping
for the life that was
for lives lost
a future of uncertainty.

You spread out
and Ghouta goes
wherever you go.

Ghouta, you did not die.
You grew, flowered under brutality
drew together, loved each other
a shining light in adversity.
And those you love, who died
wait for you above
a chorus of thousands singing you on.

Ghouta is not dead.

Garden in the ruins: Syria

Among the ruins, he grew flowers.

Shattered houses, daily bombing, death.
There, among ruined buildings
his heart of hope created a haven
for all to share.
He planted flowers on roundabouts
to cheer the battered city.
His young son worked with him.

Now
he has gone the way of his friends
gardens all destroyed
his son alone, wandering.

It is my prayer
that transient hidden beauty
among bombed buildings
behind ruined walls
stark contrast to destruction around
refuge from fear and turmoil
will comfort that young man's heart…

memories of a father who loved flowers
and grew hope.

Beneath Syrian streets

Beneath the streets
below bombs and dust and death
a quiet place, a hidden space
of books.

He works each day
collecting books, caring for books…
fourteen years old.

Children, dodging soldiers and bombs
creep through the battered streets
down the stairs, into a world of words.

A young face of love and hope
death and destruction could not extinguish.

Beneath the streets
below the dying city
a cherished hidden library
in the midst of war
a seed of future renewal.

Now all are gone
those children and the books
but, if they live on in those young hearts
there is at least one sweet memory…
in the midst of death there was refuge
in books.

One small dot

Wide, dry expanse of sculptured sand.
No man's land.
One small dark dot
moving slowly
nearing slowly.

A little child, alone
in this wild, desolate expanse
he trudges on through heavy sand
one foot, then another.
Where is his father, his mother?

Border guards meet him
take him to safety

His mother died. He came on alone
carrying a plastic bag – food, water?
No…his mother's clothes.

What did she teach him, his mother?
No matter what happens, go on, go on
towards the setting sun.
He obeyed, doggedly trudged on
alone
carrying her clothes.

The heavens weep

Raindrops trace a slow path
down my windscreen
skies crying for children's sorrow
their sad, empty tomorrow.
The heavens weep.

Grey sleet whips across the sky
a day of cold and misery
hopelessness and sorrow
for their unknown tomorrow.
The heavens weep.

My land of hope and opportunity
descending from justice and equality
from honour and democracy
into shame and ignominy.
The heavens weep.

For each one lost, deserted in their need
we sow a poisonous, an alien seed
to spawn destruction in years to come
erode our laws and bring our children harm.
What have we done?

For many it is now too late
but thousands still await their fate
each an individual, valuable, unique.
How can we wait, silent and weak?
The heavens weep.

That shameful day: April 2018

That sad, sad day
the High Court threw innocent lives away
legal it seems, but not right.
Australia descending into evil night.
We must fight, fight
not allow our laws to be changed
for political expedience, rearranged.
Not just. Not right.

Wake up, wake up Australia.
Watch out, the rot will creep in
future precarious, foundations crumbling.
Wake up. Stand up and fight
or our rights will evaporate, changed
for our leaders' convenience.

Too busy? Tired of all the fuss?
Human beings just like us
who bleed, weep, love their children
mourn their lost, suffering lands
are in a dreadful situation
dying hopes, demeaned, degraded
suffering at Australia's hands.

Stand up, at least, for the little ones
imprisoned, assaulted, intimidated.
We can't forget while one is still there
suffering in our dreadful prison camps.

Migration Amendment (Clarification of Jurisdiction) Bill 2018,
Australian Human Rights Commission http://tiny.cc/mly6cz

After High Court Decision, April 2019

Another sad day, and Lord, you say
trust in you, and I do, but
so do many of those adrift on the sea
so do many detained unendingly
who pray for their children to be free.

What can I do?
The powerful add daily to their power
the powerless lose rights hour by hour
while we fear to stand and speak
lest we be sent down with the weak
and yet, today, if all who weep combine
we could turn our land to a better way.

Lord, I know, evil does not come from you
you love each weak and struggling one
each dispossessed and homeless one
each abused and abusing one.
What can I do?

Lord, stir the hearts of thousands more
so our country hears a mighty roar
holding our leaders to account
to humanity, honesty, transparency
welcoming refugees to our shore.

Lord, here we are, your voice, your hands.
Help us make a stand
reclaim the tattered heart of this mighty land.

Present pain

Now
despair
destruction
perversion
child's life
distorted
future
impacted
twisted
hope
crushed.

Past time
long past time
to turn
but we can
we can
we can learn.

But when?
When?
realisation
remorse
change of direction.
When?

Obscene!

Children in cages, chain wire, barbed wire
cages for dogs or foxes, cages of fear.
Unbelievable. Obscene.

Yes, there is false news.
We must use reputable sources
but evidence irrefutable, undeniable
daily, planes roaring over, bombs falling
leaving more bleeding, broken, dying
children's silent screams, silenced screams
and who sent the bombs?
Who?
Who paid for the tanks and planes?

Children without childhoods taught to hate
children covered in ash and blood
obscene!
Unless we march, wave signs and scream
No more! No more! Stop the war!
Let them know peace again
this seething tide will turn, engulf us
poison our children's minds and dreams
and we will reap what we have sown.

Unless we make a stand
we sentence our land
our own children
to a history unclean.

For the Rohingya

Heavy heavy heavy
the load of sad stories…
sickness weighs me down.
What can I do?

Yours, ever-present fear
panic when a child's not near
dread at what is yet ahead
sorrow for those lost or dead
small hope, hopeless hope
that one day, one day
a friend, a parent
a lost child will reappear
from those long, silent years
and if that child should come
will she be spirit broken, numb
soul shrivelled by abuse
nothing more to lose?

Life goes on, much as before
degradation, losses raw
and always uncertainty
– watching, running, hiding
and not knowing.

Behind your eyes, always pain.

Shamim

late 2018

Shamim, where are you now?

Still in prison on Nauru
or moved secretly away?
Where are you today?

Each day, in my mind's eye
I see your face
hear your gentle voice.
Every day I pray for you.
You are part of the joy that lifts me
and the grief that weighs me down.

Shamim, you spoke so moderately
respectfully, reasonably
asking only to be free
for education
and peace with your family.

Shamim
Your mother must be proud of you.
I pray you are still together
I pray for those sweet companions
I saw with you on Facebook.

I believe even though you suffer
and your body is not free
your spirit is and always will be.

Hold on, Shamim, hold on.

No logic

I don't understand.
Contradictions everywhere
questions floating in the air
absolutely illegal and unfair
no logic, no consistency.
How can this happen?

Let's adjust this law a bit
slip in a new clause here or there
screw the thumb screws tighter
perhaps some water torture
impose maximum inconvenience
in any petty little ways
prevent comfort.

Sadistic, pulling wings off butterflies
twisted, devising ways to give pain.
Can't let them start to hope again!
Can't have anyone feel comfortable
that would never do!

To save deaths at sea
we must punish others
quash, denigrate, terrorise.
And so our selfish, phobic leaders
constantly readjust migration laws
to create maximum frustration.

It takes a special kind of brain
to create conditions like these
in our concentration camps,
inventive, but mostly sick, and thick
destroying their own reputation
and dirtying Australia's name.

And what does our own law say?
Separating families is OK?
Don't we honour the concept of family
prosecute parents who neglect children?
How can our leaders dare, dare
to even think of forcing parents
to sign away their child?

I think you'll find, in psychological interpretations
social workers' mantras and mission statements
the best place for children is with loving family
so how can politicians justify adjusting legislation
and our government's continued manipulation
of children in custody?

Heart aflame with rage, brain spinning in frustration
helpless, outraged, unbelieving
I can't understand the leaders of our nation
but I know, beyond a doubt
we must stand up for the helpless any way we can.

Amendments Again? 2018

2015 – amendments to migration act
2016 – tightening loopholes again
2017 – *'powers unlimited*
to knowingly inflict maximum discomfort'
Can you believe it? Enshrining injustice in our laws
Now, without notice, refugees moved offshore
couples separated, children imprisoned.
Our politicians flex their claws – our claws.

Can this happen in this land of opportunity?
Opportunity to debase, mistreat with impunity?
Opportunity to inflict unacceptable cruelty
illegal in our society, but OK for refugees?

Read parliament's records it if you dare
if you can bear to see the corruption there.
We share the guilt unless we each raise our voice
calling for accountability. Make your choice!

If each one of us would stir ourselves
inform ourselves, speak for the oppressed
be watchful every day, not dream comfortably on
Australians could lift their heads again.
It's up to you and me, not a nebulous 'they'
for we empower them if we do not speak.

Do these recent amendments speak for you?
They do not speak for me and so you see
I must object, or lose my integrity.

www.legislation.gov.au/Series/C1958A00062 28/Dec/2018
www.aph.gov.au/Parliamentary_Business/Bills_Legislation/bd/…
/19bd0 Feb 11, 2019

Dark-eyed girl

Young woman with intent gaze
dark eyes, sweet smile
you remind me of children dear to me
far away.

Child of the Rohingya
eyes window to heart fervent
full of curiosity
dreams and hopes
your life before you.

Dark-eyed girl
peering through the wires
Sweet, respectful voice
asking only education
and freedom.

Your face is a page of history
and the future.

Sleeping giant

Lord, forgive, forgive our gullibility
fear of involvement. We tried not to see
inhumanity perpetrated in Australia's name…
our shame.

Now the sleeping giant of uncertain voters
once timid and biddable, trusting and leadable
is stretching, listening, learning
aware now of carefully constructed disguise
contradictions of our own stand on human rights
child abuse and domestic violence.
Yes, yes, yes, we will for fight those here
Australian citizens deserve the best.

But what about the rest?

Can't politicians see, can't their supporters see
we are descending into anarchy?

Open your eyes.
See the gradual demonisation
the cruel rejection of helpless fellow humans.

Sleeping giant, it's time to rise.

Playing games?

Someone up there, high above me
living in freedom
is playing a game
throwing dice, laughing, drinking.
OK, you win, mate!
The markers are moved.
That's me, the helpless refugee
the pawn without a name.
You casually decide my fate
with your careless game.

Someone is having a tantrum
stamping and shouting
You don't do what I say.
You get in my way.
Just wait, I will get you. I'll pay you back!
My fate decided by angry children.

I hold on, I rise through trauma and sickness
still me, I survive, try to care for the others
appeal to the world for my forsaken people
illegally imprisoned, inhumanely treated
pawns in a game, a terrible game
ruled by greed, pride and desire for power.

So because I survive, stand tall despite all
try to open the world's eyes and heart
because I am unbroken, outspoken
now will you punish me for my resilience
and others like me, who desired only to join you
work with you, contribute as free, fellow citizens?

What will be the end of this sad, shameful story?

Death of a spirit

(2018: photo of a fierce little girl on Nauru)

Glaring out at the hostile world
won't eat, won't drink, fierce, implacable anger.
Inhumanity surrounds her, known only by number
what can she do but retreat into self?

Will help come, not too late for her darkening spirit
her battered, angry, retreating spirit?
Too late and a terrorist is born.
Are you proud, satisfied, all who shut your eyes
undeniable evidence denied, blindly blame, demonise?
There is no queue, there is no queue, no queue
no orderly, legal way to escape from injustice
from systematic extermination, ethnic cleansing
bombs, mother's violation, baby brother's blood.

No hope in sight, this small girl radiates hate
spirit shrivelling, childhood dying.

Bring the children here
bring them all here
so we can warm them with love
try to thaw that angry heart
those many bruised and angry hearts
until they can be children again.

Little brown boy

Little brown boy
cheeky grin
belligerent chin.
Trouble, I thought…
judged him.
Next day at the shops
there he was with mum
smiling, sweet
her little son.

Too many, seen negatively
quickly blamed, expected to fail
later in city watch house
hiding confusion and fear
behind 'I don't care.'

Unnecessary, wasteful, unfair.

Expect the best
give respect and time
hard sullen eyes
will once more shine
and there he is –
mother's little boy again.

Never alone

(for advocates, frustrated and worn)

So much pain, so much, too much.
I am wrung out with their suffering.
Too long they wait in fear and pain
too long we wait for our country's awakening.

A tsunami of weeping, groaning fills my ears
twists bowels and heart. I am torn apart
by my small suffering, and they
displaced, waiting, bear so much more.
How can they endure?

What can I do? One voice, one heart bleeding
the endless tide of wrong so strong, never ending?
How can I not weep and bleed with them?

Rest now, my child, regain your strength
while I labour on through other hearts and hands.
Retreat, sleep. I know each tear, yours and theirs.
Rest, then rise again to the endless task.
I will restore your light to once more shine
in one small corner at a time.

Our Lord knows our weaknesses, our tears.
He places a task in front of each of us
so we can be His heart and hands
walk with others in their dark days and years.

Remember, my child, I have a back-up plan.
A hidden army works and weeps with you
and while you stand back, someone new
will pick up the baton, and run in your place.

Fear in the night

(2018)

I wake, gasping for breath
Light on, sit up, breathe slow
a big decision to make
to buy a car: what age, what make?
Must be that makes me wake.

In Melbourne a father wakes, afraid
his sleeping wife and child seem safe
Then tumult, strange men break in
bind him painfully, take his child.
Mother screaming, baby screaming.
Surely they will return her
surely it's a mistake
panic rising in their throats.
Will she be harmed
will we see her again?

Unrealistic? False news?
Search official documents leaked
Border Force policy, there is no doubt
this is happening in our land.
Trust police, Border Force, the system?
But this trust has been often broken
laws adjusted, whittling away freedoms
justice continually denied.

So breath shortens, confused, afraid
unable to understand, still hoping, hoping

Imagine, a night raid, your small child taken?

Tender Age Shelters: 19.5.18

Another day, another unbelievable story.
Strong nations rise on humble people's struggles
– of course always some hidden corruption
some serious issues demanding attention –
but still honoured, respected nations.
Now someone up high, some group with power
says *Let's create a new horror, make someone suffer.*
Or *Here's another way we can punish migration!*
Then a new phrase leaps out screaming –
Tender Age Shelters for migrant children.

Meanwhile, good, established citizens
in patriotism sing anthems of glory
celebrate heroes, achievements, victories
and while they stand there, hearts swelling
immigrant children, political pawns,
infants from loving arms literally torn
from those who embarked on this odyssey
for their children's future, trusting democracy…
gone, gone into the faceless system
stealthily transported into inhospitable desert
to new gulags – Tender Age Shelters –
to suffer, swelter, punished for existence.

Flag flies, band plays, nationalism swells
confident in the right of the nation
created in its present manifestation
by early waves of the fleeing, downtrodden
(their own grandparents, have they forgotten?).
Nation built on the land of others
past wrongs still unrecognised, unrighted
original inhabitants still victimised.

Are sadists simply seeking satisfaction
refugee children convenient scapegoats…
democracy regressing into depths of injustice.

Another supposedly democratic nation
accepted families slowly hopeful, relaxing
children's nightmares at last fading
working, paying taxes, though still limited rights
grateful, contributing then, door knock in the night!
All wake in fright (déjà vu: this happened before
forcing exodus from their own loved shore)
once again, terror, seizure, transportation.

Is this my nation, with boundless plains to share?
Advance Australia Fair – to where?
Down into depths of repression, injustice?
Recreating the dark ages, reimposing terror
under the guise of protecting our nation
stockpiling shame for the next generation.

Now, that off my mind, I have voiced my pain
can I relax, the children even now waking
in a barren place, bewildered and frightened?
Now as I drink my coffee, sit in the sun
refugees, legally seeking a home
are sent back to the terror they fled.
After all, what is the value of one life?
and one more and one more?

www.usatoday.com/story/news/politics/…tender-age-shelters…
/716749002/

The tide will turn

The tide runs in relentlessly
and it must run its course
then it will turn and flow again
into deep sea.
The tide has run in destructively
and now I pray it's time to change
flow back to humanity.

Surely the horrors now must end
the oppressors turn
see the error of their ways
the wreckage wrought
clear the veil from their eyes
so all can learn
that oppressed and oppressors all
are humankind.

The evil tide that has defiled our land
now must obey the moon
return to its home
so, very soon
the tide of cruelty and hate
must surely turn
…must surely turn.

My inspired new solution
(2018)

Just think, if we had saved all the money spent
on court cases forcing urgent intervention
on wasteful management of detention
on hiding the sordid facts from Australians
millions siphoned away, unaccounted-for
deals that have failed, money doubly wasted
the money of Australian taxpayers
of former refugees, the mainstay of our nation...

if we had saved all that, we would have plenty
to help solve homelessness, improve Newstart
mend horrific Aboriginal youth detention
develop natural energy, or regeneration
of our damaged reefs, farmland and forests
and ironically
many refugees have skills to aid the solution.
Already we benefit from those settled here

And have you forgotten one other small thing?
Most of us come from a refugee ancestry.

What an intricate web of waste and dirty dealing
what a jungle of secrecy and criminal collusion
those who want to reach out unable to break free
from the network of handshakes, deals, secrecy.
Australia's reputation ridiculed and dirtied,
our helpless victims still illegally tortured
children not knowing freedom and education
their childhood spent
in the polluted atmosphere of our offshore prisons.

So what do you think of my 'new' solution:
bring them all here – a win-win situation
stop throwing money into a limitless black hole
gain valuable new citizens
who have proven their positive attitudes, non-violence
then we can use taxpayers' money where intended
begin to redeem our damaged reputation.

Just bring them all here
then we can begin respectful processing
of thousands more who hoped to reach our shore
turned back, towed back, warehoused in Indonesia
still endlessly suspended in detention there
and with nearby nations we can face our obligation
to find them all a home.

Bring them here, don't wait for another self-immolation
for more deterioration, arguments, litigation.
It is legally enacted, why more waiting?

Just bring them all here.

Dare you?

Dare you step into the wild…
fallen trees, debris of shattered lives
careers, reputations dirtied
minds seduced by tempting lies
impenetrable thorned vines
in the wilds of human minds?

Scams and dirty deals thrive
in deep gloom beneath the trees
truth obscured, entangled, tied
in vindictive legislation.
Corruption's tentacles cling
deadly virus creeping in
mould and decay, sad evidence
of honesty decaying, truth eroding
our once great, respected nation
sinking into the swamp.

Wake up, clear mind, open eyes!
Cut back the vines, entanglements
that cloud brain, obscure thoughts
insincere praise disguised as truth
(can't you smell the rot?).
Soon you will see new tender shoots
of truth thrust through
compassion struggle towards the light
regrowth of lost innocence.

We can tame the wild.

One ordinary person

(February 2019)

Me, one weak person
far from you, unknown to you
what can I do?
I rage and weep and pray
write to politicians, sign petitions
hold you in my heart night and day
but you are there, so far away
in pain, fear and uncertainty
watching your children in agony
as they negotiate their sad, weary way
through childhood.

My well of tears for you is deep
you are in always in my mind
travel with me wherever I go.
I am worn by my anger
with mourning for your daily pain
my strength spent in sorrow.

How must you feel?

Tears for the Hazara

Between, cast out, nowhere in front of me
behind, desolation, pain and not knowing.

Where are they now: old uncle, my mother
little sister, children of dead brother?
I came ahead in desperate need
to survive, prepare a place, succeed
bring them from where death stalks each day
so I struggled towards a safe place
through endless mountains, hostile lands
hoping, trusting in a welcome there.
Meanwhile, that Eden shut its gates
imprisoned me here to wait, wait
in hardship, injustice and indignity
in an atmosphere of cruelty and hate.

If I were free, I could prepare a place
for any who escape, longing to be free
contribute to my new community
help those in distress. But I am not free.

So my aged mother weeps.
She had prayed I would be free
a beacon of hope through her sterile days.
Where is she: stumbling in the dark
hiding in ruins in my sad, torn land
starving, tending mutilated children?

My harassed, hunted people, my dear country
I can give you no hope. I also am adrift
in a merciless sea of inhumanity.

Refugee mother to her child

How can I tell you to hope, my child?
Hope is gone
shrivelled up on this bare, caustic stone.

For years I've tried to keep your hope alive
told of a future where we could live in peace
part of a free community
told you good stories of the past
before rockets' annihilation, bombs' blast
of times of harvest, of festivity
you treasured, secure on grandfather's knee.

Tell me again, Mama, tell me again.

I hid my tears, my horror at the reality
of ethnic cleansing
to give you happy memories, and hope
dreams of new beginnings
but now my own hope has almost died.
I see no way
nothing beyond this fearful day.

My little one
my sad, old, little one
I have no happy words
no hope to give.

Port Ashmore: a comedy?

2002: new law
Ashmore Reef to become a port.
And what is there? No port of any sort
but legally a port!

Why such strange manipulations?
Intercepted refugees
intentionally, cunningly
brought through Ashmore Reef
entering Darwin legally, they thought
were therefore not
as Darwin was their second port.

Years pass. Imprisoned, lives on hold
and it was a mistake

2017: Federal Court declared those laws
never finalised, so in honesty
(fair go, mate)
we will retrospectively
recognise those refugees
1,600 refugees, legally
and compensate.
It's clear to me.

But now these laws
declared not laws by Federal Court
are legalised retrospectively
the prisoners still illegal entrants
though illegally detained
their detention a lie.

July 20, 2018 we read
law corrected retrospectively
refugees status not corrected
the injustice remains
very very strange.

Detailed report on Ashmore Reef
reasons for needing a port
requirements, responsibilities
'Quarantine instructions, hull inspections'
'high risk of marine encrustations
unacceptable risks for terrestrial and marine life'.

I wonder, were those inspections done
on ships bringing in refugees
where there was no port, no staff
just reefs, usually under water?

In circumventing Refugee Conventions
perhaps
Border Force itself broke quarantine laws?

Legally illegal intervention?

www.theguardian.com/.../1600-asylum-claims-could-be-reopened-due-to-poorly-...

Forced removal, again

(2 December 2018)

Harsh, stark
Manus camp
dry, hot
water cut off.
Water, water
just one cup
in his name?

Shame, shame
on Australia's name.

Last memento
letter, photo
gone, torn
nothing left.
Why? Why destroy?

Bereft…
wife died far away
my children
where are they?
I don't know…
phone taken
no contact
my children
alone, alone
and I alone
last photo gone
gone, all gone.

At Christmas

When will your suffering cease?
your hearts know peace
when will our shame end?
It seems daily to increase

This heavy load upon my heart
I share by choice, in some small part.
How can I not feel your pain?
We are fellow humans, though far apart.

Lord, take today's load of grief.
I give you my anger, my disbelief
only You are strong enough
to carry it all and give relief.

Tomorrow and tomorrow
another load of pain.
How can we wash away the stain?
Help me to do what little I can
then trust the load to you again.

Frozen Rose

Her face haunts me
dark eyes deep with sorrow
pleading on the screen.

Over 5 years I watched her
in groups of incarcerated children
sweet face, warmth and grace
asking only freedom and education
no blame, no recriminations
slowly growing from graceful bud
to frozen rose.

Years pass, hope fades, fades, goes.
A young woman now, in her eyes no pleading
only faint, resigned hope, and cold sorrow.
In the hot hell of Nauru, a frozen rose.

Where is she now?
Perhaps, Nauru behind her
perhaps in USA
information scarce.

I pray her heart will again warm and glow.

Another new year

Another new year.
As I sit here contemplating
vines dancing in morning breeze
my spirit reaches over wide seas
seeking yours
to strengthen you.

May hope clothe you once again
despite disruptions and indignities
daily disrespect and pain.

I send to you, I pray for you
the balm of green things growing
quiet time for privacy and peace
to heal and dream,
cover you gently with my thoughts
as a mother covers a sleeping child.
Rest, rest.

In my quiet time of meditation
receive my gift, be blessed
with an inner haven in your soul
despite sad memories
inhumanities.

I pray hope to you,
Keep it glowing in your heart.

Beyond imagining

In so many places, many still unknown
such cruelty, pain and despairing
new crises daily, thousands wait, suspended
people like me, with hopes for their children
people like you, running from violence.
Wouldn't I? Wouldn't you?

Each father trying to care for his family
each mother, love and pain in her heart
each child, much like yours, like mine
perhaps, in his eyes, her eyes, hope still shines
perhaps her mother soothes her with lies…
Of course Australia would love a child like you
of course we will have a safe home one day…

Beyond imagining, the weight of fear
heap of dying hopes rising, insurmountable
uncertainty beyond my imagining

My lord, You know each fear, each tear.
Move the nations to open their hearts
and never let us stop crying and trying
for people like us, our brothers and sisters
fellow humans
who trusted us for justice.

Homeless

Whose child is this who lies
mute, plundered, dissected
(grandfather's nose, mother's eyes)?

Child, where is your mother?
Has she forgotten you
does she know where you are?

In the womb, they say
the child recognises the parent's voice
feels pain, senses moods
moves to music.

This child so still on the slab
is homeless, the womb denied
no comforting heartbeat
no encompassing warmth.
But aren't there children's rights
detailed, enforced, defended?

There are funds
campaigns
for the rights of homeless
caseworkers, agitators, legislators…
a Year of the Homeless!

Child, lying cold on the slab
where is your mother?
Does she know where you are?

In future years, will she grieve for you?

Through the night

Through the night rain falls down
caressing earth and sea and town
and in the sound I hear the pain
of conflicts past, and then again
the silent roar of passing years
conflicts, separations, tears.

I feel the chill and misery
of homeless people on the sea
the hopelessness, helplessness
of bewildered, fleeing refugees.

Through the night, rain falls down
gently on land and sea and town
and in the sound is comfort's song
for families gathered safe at home
blotting out sad voices of the lost
struggling, hunted, tempest-tossed
the loneliness, the emptiness
of the battered and bereaved
their pain of separation from
a homeland they must leave.

Lord, bring them to a friendly shore
where they can live in peace once more
beneath their own roof, safe and warm
sheltered at last from life's fierce storm
listening to a friendly rain
blessing their own roof again.

Climate change

Our climate has changed.
Self-interest and political gain shame our nation.

Are these the death throes of humanity?
Tortured souls fleeing annihilation
in terror and hope leaving loves and home
over hostile, unknown lands to roam
seeking a place where their children can be safe.
For this, demonised, right of sanctuary denied,
our nation step by step desensitised.

Our sad world needs our voices to speak out.
It's our responsibility
to realign slipping standards and priorities
increase awareness of conditioning.
(Have I been blindfolded, wooed gently
in a direction foreign to the me I used to be?)

Australia, wake up, break the apathy, passivity
revitalise decency, soften hearts desensitised
Or will we still sit back? I am only one.
What can be done by one?

Perhaps someone is watching me, watching you…
waiting to dare and change with you.
We can't plead ignorance – evidence of brutality
leaps from Facebook and TV for all the world to see
Who can say *I did not know. None of this relates to me.*
How can we deny promises broken, climate of secrecy
while children are suffering, decency dying?

Now is the hour to turn the tide, begin the transition
back from climate of secrecy and brutality
shake off shackles of fear, stand up for homeless
brutalised, needlessly institutionalised
fight for climate cleansing – now!

Come together. Draw strength from each other
stand up for downtrodden sister and brother
embrace the privilege of hospitality
the responsibility that comes with prosperity.

Together we can make the climate change.

Anyone watching?

A new refugee prison in Melbourne
bare, sterile, well walled. What is it for?
Surely not a welcoming place
where the victimised can at last relax
heart and health restore?
Psychologists would suggest
gardens, running water, healing space.

What is it for, this foreboding place?
Must we wait until spirits and hopes die
then bring them here, legal refugees
and lock them in prison again?
Why not act sooner, save millions
save spiritual destruction, years of pain
waste of time, of valuable contributions
of new citizens, enriching our society?
Why all the waste?

Where are the checks, accountability?
Generous donations to restore our reef
thoughtfully researched of course
– by whom, and donations to whom?
For what purpose specifically
where accounted for? Evidence please.

Why are we, a supposedly democratic society
becoming more brutal, secretive
the rich obscenely richer, the poor, poorer?
If we wait, we vote for the status quo.
It's up to you and me to model accountability
insist on honesty.

Should I intrude?

In every place are homes and families
living lives the tourist cannot see.
As I pass, I glimpse some of these and wonder.

Child on the beach alone, staring out to sea
homeless young man sleeping under a tree
old woman gathering cans stoically
– each has a story.

Shall I try to make some connection
broach barrier of chosen isolation
of poverty, discrimination?
Better to pass by?

No, I will, I must risk intrusion
if only so just one more lonely person
perhaps seeming to prefer seclusion
knows someone cared.

Perhaps
the child now is laughing with family
the derelict in warm community
the environmentalist satisfied with her tally.
I'll never know…

or perhaps my smile made one heart glow
caused warm, healing tears to flow
made a difference.

Money, money, money

More and more money
flamboyantly thrown
spent in many directions.
Smokescreen, cunning planning
to obscure future schemes
cover failures, past disasters.

Add up the millions ostentatiously scattered
to distract attention from serious matters
A crisis? Polls dropping? Rats leaving?
More money will fix it, another big splash
more taxpayers' dollars to divert detractors
make it look like we're being governed.

Millions disappear, no proper tendering
'We are all powerful!
We hold the purse strings!
Trust us. We know best!'
Cut pensions, cut services
drop successful programmes
so we can throw more millions
in the black hole of corruption
and political desperation.

The people are waking
wondering, demanding.
You have holed your own boat
cut your own throat.
Your reckless ride is soon ending.

False news?

Though you might try to convince our trusting nation
our prison camps are similar to holiday resorts
that 'they' themselves are to blame for all their suffering
 – after all, just because they were persecuted
saw their children killed, families decimated
babies thrown in to the fire – even so
just because a father was tortured for speaking
their mother, their sister raped before their eyes
homes burned, fields razed, education forbidden
simply for being a Yadzi, Hazara, Rohingya
for generations now harried, expelled, tortured
 – still
what right have such people to come here for help
with their tortured memories and traumatised children?

Then, after years of captivity and degradation
they wilfully get sick or self-harm to get attention
to blackmail Australia into action?

So, all those photos, videos of guards abusing
eyewitness accounts, news from international bodies
are just manufactured to make trouble
all false news?

Are we so gullible?
I don't think so.
Is Australia waking up?
Surely we must.

Seesaw and swings

Try the roundabouts, try the swings
up and down on the seesaws
whichever brings the most degradation
never mind shame heaped on our nation.

Teeter totter wobbling, swing chains rusting
people waking, realising, objecting?
Well, let's shift the draughtsmen
cause distraction with illogical action
move to Nauru and Manus
to hospital, then back again
no treatment, health worsening
Anything to win votes, spread false news

Costly deals with Malaysia, USA, Cambodia,
(of course never New Zealand)
now another flamboyant, regressive, complicating
money-wasting, impromptu, knee-jerk reaction
– move them back to Christmas Island again.

Smiles and pontifications, kiss all the babies
support many new causes, any new causes
– election coming!

I am sorry for you, trying so desperately
clumsily, to hide your desperation.
What a waste of talents, human resources.
What a waste of millions, of privilege, of time
revealing your incompetence to all the nation.
What a waste!

To a baby boy

2019

My little one, so beautiful, trusting me
mine the scary privilege
to guide, set an example
establish useful boundaries
of good living, honesty.
Your health is my responsibility
so, limits on sugar, fast food
bedtime suitable for your age.
Your potentiality trusted to us
your parents, or carers.
You are very small and we know best.

We will not fence you in with harsh laws
but within safe limits, let you experience
feel the consequences of disobeying rules
results of greed, of late nights.
We will model values for you
affirm you in obedience
our task while you are so young
your life hardly begun.
We know what is best or you.

My sweet child, gentle and kind.
A new thought comes to my mind.
Would you rather be a girl, my son?
We have no daughter, we won't mind.
It's up to you.
You know best.

Child sacrifice

All hail the god of luxury
of selfishness and freedom
the God of 'me'.
I am entitled to the best
I come first no matter what
doesn't matter about the rest.
Anyone standing in my way
is an annoying pest
to be exterminated without delay
a sacrifice to the God of freedom.

This thing that grew in me
knew my voice
comforted by my heartbeat
a child I thought would fill a need
someone to always love me
perhaps an accessory
– *me and my beautiful child* –
well, I've changed my mind.

Grandma's hair, her father's eyes
perhaps my nose, your funny toes
and in her mind
deep attachment to my heartbeat
my laugh, my voice she knows.

I've changed my mind
I have the right to decide
– my body, my choice.
Little one, for you no voice
for you torture, dismemberment…
for you, no choice.

It's beginning!

Now it's beginning – the young are rising
fighting for their future. We must join them.
Vibrant young people, sincere, convinced
safeguarding our futures, daring to challenge
erosion of integrity, corruption and secrecy.

And do you realise, forward 20 years
(time warp, shapeshift)
this joyful harvest, flowering of our society
could be decimated, many long dismembered
tortured in the womb, murdered at birth
inconvenient, unwanted and, even more sickening
trafficked as spare parts –
commercialising babies' bodies?

So, in the near future if these practices continue
young, fervent defenders of our rights, our planet
would be much fewer
the young, idealistic
won't be here to fight for us
– macabre justice!

Our suffering country, more and more denuded
desecrated, poisoned, because we allowed
the reign of dark forces, gods of greed, cruelty.

A final, sad irony: by perverted choice
murdering our next generation
who would probably grow to be
our struggling earth's salvation.

Ageing

Long spell of ill-health
sitting by my window contemplating…

Losses upon losses
skills lessening, abilities fading
importance diminishing
powers sliding away.
falling one by one, autumn leaves
loss of role, of consequence.
Is there an antidote for these?

Long-held causes, dearly loved
slipping into other hands
or voluntarily, lovingly passed on
evolving, changing inevitably.

Was it all in vain
…my heartfelt contributions?
Doubts rise. Shall I hold grief close
keep sorrows warm
or let go gracefully?

There are rewards as life slows
time to write, to sit and dream
freedom to follow a new path
losses softening, hopefully
into pleasant memories.

Each chapter brings possibilities
My heart aches for the many
feeling obsolete, discarded.

I can still post and sign.

Unwanted

Indistinct movement flutters vaguely.
She is waving
from isolated, barred window
across barbed wire and sterile cement.

Who is she, alone, unvisited?
An aged woman, suffering dementia
waiting, waiting deportation.

Who will speak for her?
Who cares?

Asylum seekers, recognised refugees
imprisoned across the yard
plead for her, for care, for kindness.
Result: her window is covered
even that small contact denied
now no sky, no clouds, no view
no distant human figures across the yard
waving to her.

Unknown and unwanted
forgotten, except by the repressed
imprisoned near her
their concern for her forbidden.

Their sin
to flee repression, seek safety.
Hers, to grow old

War for our world: March 2019

Ominous drumbeat, distant searchlights, flares
rumblings and tremors, the earth creaks, ripples
years of spying, planning reaches fruition
long hidden cocoons, extraterrestrial spawn
burst forth. Daleks rise armed and ready.
Tripods, oil rigs, oil barons and frackers
stride closer, towering over the land
seeking to subjugate and plunder.

Can't you hear dark music, feel earth trembling?
We must all unite or face certain destruction
and the earth we know will be unrecognisable.

The Gurawa of Borroloola cry out against fracking
desecration of ancient sites, of water, of habitats
cry for our help in the coming combat.
On the Bight, people meet to stand for clean seas.
As whales play, unknowing the probable future
far east the reef weeps waiting more destruction
as poisonous sediment from mining's deep fracking
covers and suffocates coral formations
kills the unique creatures sheltering there.

The insatiable gods of riches and power
nourished by false news, fear and hysteria
grow stronger, consuming, digesting, possessing
more and more of our agonised land.
Too long we have waited, passive and silent
while enemies soothe and seduce our leaders.

We have failed to protect vulnerable ecosystems
to safeguard our own children's future.
Now, perhaps, one last opportunity.

The children are rising, prepared and determined
to unite, to march, to campaign for their future.
We must fight with them, use all our weaponry
slow our country's slide to destruction.
Schoolchildren mobilising, grandmas and more
to fight for clean air, clean seas, for the wildlife
all these gifts we have taken for granted
while pollution grew to an epidemic.
Now stand firm, Australians, fight the invaders
or our descendants will not know this land's wonders
but some sad, broken parody we'd hardly recognise.

Music grows louder, the monsters stalk nearer
gunfire and siren wail, louder and clearer.
This horror movie is your life and mine
unless... Yes, we have the antivenene
to kill off the monsters: they have no resistance
to unity and honesty, their anathema.

Come, let's unite all races, all colours
scientists, dreamers, all genders, religions
each one has a skill or talent to add
to overcome the false, cruel gods of greed
halt the destruction before it's too late
so this wonderful earth can rest and start healing
so our children and all future generations
can enjoy the wonders of this awesome creation.

Will I let you live?

There you are on the ultrasound
stretching, bending
standing tall, then slipping down
kicking off again, straightening
exercising enthusiastically
and is that a smile I see?

Besides the bump, shortness of breath
and you eternally rippling my abdomen
you are manageable, contained
but later
you will control my days
all corners of my life
needing feeding, cleaning, clothing.

Do I really want all that?
Limitations, less time for partying
less money for stylish clothes?
Hmm…
inconvenient?

Do I really want you in my life?

Medevac Bill passed!

20.3.2019

Third of February, a great day
– at last the Medevac Bill is passed!
Collective sigh, justice at last!
Now, another day, another day
another week, nothing done.

The Bill was passed, we celebrated
the promise to bring the sick here now
and almost all are sick on Manus
infected by our representatives
as surely as if they were injected
intentionally, with hopelessness.

Unbelievable. Inconceivable.
Australia, a democracy
signatory to welcome refugees.
Justice again scorned, ignored.

Another day, another day of pain
urgently needing medical attention.
Just what is your intention
– a pure white, pseudo-Christian nation?
You, in control of immigration
of visas and necessary exemptions
you, who have power to act today
what is the plan?
Create your ideal society?

You can act with speed
when it suits your needs
to hide your team's misdeeds
so what are your intentions here?
It's getting horrifyingly clear
you care for no one but your own.

You present reasons for impeachment
disbarment, at least replacement
and still you smile and scheme.
Now, opening Christmas Island again
an expensive step back in time
simply stalling, hoping all refugees will die?

Do you hate your own land so much
the Australia you claim to protect
to more deeply dirty our country's name
tread us down further into the mire
of shame and disgrace
down from our once-respected place?
Another day, another day gone
They could be here, should be here!

Stop the traffic, storm the Bastille
nail declaration on Parliament's door
march, waving flags, for civilisation
for humanity or just plain honesty.
Whatever it is, it must be done.

Whatever we demand
must include dignity and respect.
Bring them to a healing place
trees, streams and waiting friends
not another stark, bare prison.

Another day, another day gone
Christmas island again re-shut
expensive demonstration of power
more millions wasted, time wasted
victims, weak and ill, re-repressed
now cholera diagnosed.

Is there any logic here?
A sad, wasteful chapter in history!

You can move with speed when it suits your needs.
Another day, another weary day gone…

Morning check of Facebook

March 2019

A few tears, internal
perhaps a few external
over-emotional?
Some say so.
I weep and hurt for refugees
misguided criminals
even trees
all sorts of things
and especially for the babies
pulled limb from limb
snipped, clipped, torn
not long before time to be born.
sentient fellow humans
who feel, smile, respond.

And now even worse
in many places
legally murdered at birth
(even after birth?).

Overdoing it? Overreacting?
over-romanticising pregnancy and birth?
Before you judge me
delete or unfriend me
do you have a baby?
a loved grandchild?
Imagine that little one
in a murdered baby's place.

Imagine that sweetly formed body
dear little face...
imagine, really try
that baby torn, dismembered
crying, suffering.

Don't avoid this challenge
though sickening, distasteful.
See your own infant's face
as they pull it apart
crush skull, remove heart
perhaps harvest and sell
for spare parts.

Now, if you really, sincerely tried
to see, in reality
how are you feeling, deep inside?

Overreaction, unnecessary detail?
Gross to even discuss this so baldly?

I do not apologise.

The human condition

We look out through skewed world views
holding tight our treasure
ignoring different, difficult people
rejecting, discriminating in subtle ways
clearly seen by those watching.

The treachery and selfishness of humanity
manipulation, misinformation, confrontation
grow in apathy and fear. It could happen here!
for fear is hate and hate is fear.
It's near! It's here!
Hidden in apathy the cancer grows
unseen, unclean, obscene.

Lord, let me always feel another's pain
and weep for children's fears. Don't let me forget!
Lead the child of violence to trust again
and laugh again.

The antidote is love
knowing we are precious
let us show others they are precious
if we listen to their stories, share ourselves
respect accept all colours races sizes faces
agonise, empathise, weep and laugh with them.
You will use us to glow to show your love
into lonely hearts and fearful places.

Lord, forgive our selfishness, confusion
knit us, twine us, splice us together
a wonderful diversity of colours, sizes, faces
lifestyles, minorities – humanity.

At last!
(June 2019)

At last, all children are off Nauru.
Relief! Relax! Celebrate!
It's been a long, sad fight
planning, meeting, praying
feeling their fears, their fright.
Well done, you who agonised
posted, tweeted, demonstrated
well done but still not done…
These children, long in our hearts
have gone, moved on
to a pleasant place, to freedom,
or are they still controlled, repressed
vilified and spied upon?
Now we are powerless to help
and there's an emptiness.

One thing we do know
billed for their flight to freedom
more than the usual traveller pays
they begin again burdened by debt.
So, illegally imprisoned, disrespected
years of earning power lost
decent food, medical care denied
health impaired, perhaps destroyed
and they must again pay the cost ?

They are in prison still.

Where is my baby?

(children seized at the Mexican border)

Lost children, torn from us,
the children we fled for
so they could have a life
much better than ours – where are they?

Children bewildered, missing parents
forgetting mother's face.
Parents agonising. *Is she OK?*
Perhaps good foster-parents
who love him, love her as their own?
We don't know, we don't know.

If we could just know he's happy…
decent people, good friends…
if we knew she was loved
perhaps we could wait, hope for reunion,
but no answer, no word, silence.

Do traffickers have her? Do her carers abuse her?
My beautiful child, my own little one…
Round and round in their hearts
but no sound from the void
the vortex that swallowed the children
arms empty, children gone gone.
Gone where?

If we could only know, are they well?

My sweet little girl, your solemn boy
just like his father, so loving, so loved
our purpose, our treasure…where are they?

The stars look down

May 2019

Warm in my car I lay watching the stars
Sleep wouldn't come. Stars shone on
myriads winking and smiling at me
yet remote, beyond human frailty.

Filled with awe, I spoke long with my Lord
creator of this wide land, of the world
who placed the stars, knows each of us
our lives, our loves, our worries and pains.

I asked Him to please keep hope alive
in the hearts of suffering, downtrodden, lonely
wayward, ashamed, the wrongly blamed
those illegally, cruelly detained.

I pleaded for those imprisoned, oppressed
in our shameful camps, or detention here
for children locked up in city watch houses
young children in prison, families fractured.
(My Lord, my Lord, keep their hope alive.)

And I prayed
for the leaders who cause this injustice.
One day they will know their fearful wrongs
feel the weight of hate and fear they used
the powers for good they long abused.

Then they will be the oppressed
must accept the blame, own their shame.

I prayed that we who mean well will try harder
stand stronger, speak louder and never give up.

The serene, clean stars above listened to me
as I sent struggling up through the night
this anguished prayer for those dislocated
by greed of the powerful, wars and injustice.

Lord, use me to help one, two, or three.
While they are not free I can never be free.

Lord, who created these stars shining above
and are ready to carry our guilts and our pains
I pray for those hurting or burdened with guilt
that they trust your promise, accept your love.

If we each do our bit, there will be hope and justice
our country will climb from shame and disgrace.
Lord, give us strength to stand for the right
so Australia will regain her place in the light.

Violent times

This world rolls on, grinds on
wars after wars after wars
despairing prayers rise
bombs fall from the same skies
shutting our borders, seas, doors
to the victims
while still supporting the wars
a dreadful cycle, out of control
destroying futures
damaging our nation's soul.

One more sudoku
– that I can control –
soothing sequence, leading somewhere
moments respite from anger and stress
then
back into the sad, evil mess
trying to support those suffering
let them know someone cares.

On and on it goes
the never ending procession
illogical legislation
greed, repression
helplessness.

Alone

Leaving Sumatra again, July 2019

Kuala Namu Airport.
Through the gates, I am alone.
Life there continues. I, cut off
friends unseen, loved voices unheard.

Time to be sensible, squash dreams.
I am rich in memories
blessings heaped, heaped up
but still my heart is sick and sad.
Never to enter this land again?
How can I still my dreams, my yearning?

And so I think of you, in cruel detention.
So you felt, but deeper, more final
parting with fear and hopelessness.
I am rich in memory, in love, in family
and you cut off for long years
no reunion, no future in sight
only the wondering, yearning
sickness, humiliation, degradation.

Your children grow, unseen, in danger,
you cannot protect them.
Your mother dies alone, calling your name.
How can I grieve my little losses…
yours so overwhelming?

Please hold onto your dreams,
do not give up.
A better day for you must come.

The voice of Australia

This world is falling to pieces
slowly steadily disintegrating
so much fighting, so much hating, so much destruction.

Come on, you know the answer
– we must all speak up together
the silent must find their voices before it's too late.

Stand up for endangered species
speak against cruel live transportaion
of animals, and also of humans…so much to be done.

Stand against fracking and drilling
endangering underground water tables
march and protest for the environment…and what about refugees?

Campaign for whales and turtles
for our reef, for better air quality
for water stealing, for dying rivers…what about human babies?

Work together to prevent domestic violence
safety of women, and safety of children
against tearing unborn babies to pieces. Lift your voice!

Come on now, all stand together
for freedom of speech, and for transparency
for respect, accountability. Time is passing.

Join and all work together.
Each small voice adds volume until it's impossible to ignore
the voice of Australia.

Prayer for those in darkness

Lord, I pray for souls in darkness
hiding from reality
in darkness of hate and cruelty.
Set them free.
Lord, you know these souls in darkness
deep into their hearts you see
their fears, resentments, greed
that direct their hateful actions
discarding love for inhumanity.

Lord, I pray for those in darkness
I pray one day they will see light
know the pain and peace of caring
of doing what is just and right
seeing their own fallibility
owning their humanity.

I pity them their narrow hearts
gripped tight by distrust and fear
grieve their terrible day of truth
when they will at last see clear
past lies and scams and posturing
to the sad waste and desolation
the heavy load they have laid upon
defenceless souls in need.

Lord, I pray for those in darkness.
Give them light to see.

Unleash compassion

(A comment on Facebook: 'Unleash your compassion.')

Unleash compassion! Let it run free!
But first pull it out from under the debris
(yes, I know some use theirs constantly).
Dust it off, nurture it, feed it
exercise and stretch it
but hurry, hurry, get to work!
Compassion needed urgently
not someone else's – yours!
Don't procrastinate or shirk
let it run free, follow fearlessly.
This diseased country needs a large dose
to overcome heart blindness, fear and apathy
selfishness, self-preservation, cruelty.
Come on: unleash compassion and kindness
write, post, demonstrate
and tweet, tweet, tweet.

One little family (oh so dangerous)
lonely on Christmas Island waits your kindness
54 refugees locked up in Bomana
sick and weary, held incommunicado
though assessed as needing urgent medical care
despairing, losing hope, needing your compassion
waiting for you to put your kindness into action.

You are needed now. It's getting late.
Unleash your compassion!
Let it run free!

How can this happen?

(September 2019, watching video of forced removal of refugee family)

My Lord, my Lord
give them strength
the mother, the father
to hold on to sanity
to find a way to normalise
abnormal brutality
ease their children's fears
through their own despairing tears.

Parents powerless, children traumatised
again and again in security's name!

Hear the little ones crying!
Insanity, brutality
and more millions down the drain
just to victimise, terrorise
punish them, distance them
from any comfort and support.
There is no justification
no acceptable explanation…
cancer growing
infectious disease spreading,
democracy dying.
Around the world refugees repressed
children traumatised, humanity bleeding.

Are you weeping?

Three women of Iran

Faces of grace, intelligence, humour
faces alive with youth and promise
faces of compassion and love
vanished from sight into brutal prisons
each one sentenced to 18 long years.
They stood up for human rights.

How many more, unknown, unreported
their fruitful lives, their contributions
lost from our view and lost from their children
decaying, suffering in detention
their years of productivity wasted?

How many more, repressed and in hiding
or climbing, struggling over steep mountains
and then, after enduring long, dangerous journeys
at last almost in sight of freedom
detained for the sin of wanting to live
to be free to contribute, to bring up their children
turned back, refused their rightful asylum
now look out through razor wire longing for life
waiting, hope failing as sad years slip by.

And why? No acceptable reason or justification
no excuse for silence or turning away.
These are our sisters, our brothers, our children.
Can't you feel their despair, degradation?

Come, wake up, all stand together.
This evil disease, poisonous miasma
is growing in power, rolling towards us.

We must mobilise. Now. Today.

Inland night

Sink into my soul, wide land.
Dark night, hint of rust and dust
perhaps only because I know
the colours waiting.
Sink in.
Inland stillness
fill me with peace.

Soul of my land
I know you are there
battered, honour shredded
dirtied, shamed
by power's dark games.
Still you wait
beneath the debris
unchanged.

Sink in to sad souls
searching for somewhere
for truth and justice
your heart still strong
still welcoming.

Soul of my land, sink in
claim the persecuted
the lonely as your own.

www.ingramcontent.com/pod-product-compliance
Lightning Source LLC
Chambersburg PA
CBHW070916080526
44589CB00013B/1318